S0-BOH-989

Fishing

Written by Ann Love with Jane Drake
Illustrated by Pat Cupples

Kids Can Press

ARCHWOOD SCHOOL
800 ARCHIBALD STREET
WINNIPEG, MANITOBA
R2J 0Y4

"Oh, he's a keeper!" Grandma says. She reaches to hold Jessie's new baby brother before they're even through the door.

"What's a 'keeper'?" asks Jessie.

"An oldtimer's word for a fish worth keeping," Grandpa laughs.

Jessie sits on the front step and looks down the New Brunswick coastline. She and her mother have travelled all the way from British Columbia to visit Grandma and Grandpa and to show off her brother. She's tired and misses Dad, who couldn't come on this trip.

"I'm going to check my fish farm now," says Grandpa. "Want to come? You can choose a fish for supper."

"Sure," Jessie says. "Let's go."

3

They putt away from the wharf in Grandpa's dory. Grandpa points to a large fishing boat out in the bay.

"That's a trawler. It carries a net that opens so wide underwater it could catch a hockey rink full of fish," Grandpa shouts above the noise of the engine.

The huge net is towed behind the trawler on long cables. For years, trawl nets dragged the sea bottom, where groundfish live, and hauled up tons of cod, halibut and flounder. Too many were caught, so today groundfish are in shorter supply. A few trawlers still fish near the coast, but most have to travel far out to sea.

trawler

dory

trawl net

"See that longliner?" Grandpa points to a boat on shore. "It's not used any more."

Longliners catch groundfish near wrecks and rocks, where a trawl net might snag. While the longliner chugs forward, the crew shoots a hooked and baited groundline off the back of the boat. When the line settles on the ocean floor, groundfish bite the bait and get hooked.

With fewer groundfish left to catch, many longliners now lie abandoned, and their crews are out of work.

"Grandpa, if there aren't lots of groundfish left, what can we take home for supper?" asks Jessie.

"A tasty farmed fish," Grandpa answers.

groundline

longliner

"Some of us in the village have learned to farm fish," Grandpa explains. "We mostly grow Atlantic salmon, but I'm also trying to farm halibut. People love the way they taste, but there aren't many wild halibut to catch any more."

Fish farmers grow fish in floating sea cages that are anchored to the ocean bottom. Grandpa's farm has twelve cages strapped together and connected with walkways. Some sea cages hold small fish, others larger fish, and at least one cage holds fish big enough to sell.

Every day, workers ride their dories out to the sea cages to feed the fish. When a buyer places an order, workers catch the fish with a hand net, kill and clean them, then pack them in insulated boxes for shipping.

"But how do you get the fish to live in these cages?" Jessie asks. "And can't the little ones just swim out the holes?"

"Let's go to the hatchery and you'll see," says Grandpa.

"Fish farming begins here in a hatchery. Workers collect eggs from captive adult fish," Grandpa explains. "After the eggs hatch, the fish grow in tanks until they are big enough to sell to fish farmers like me."

Newly hatched fish are see-through and smaller than mosquitoes. In this hatchery, young halibut are kept in pails and fed tiny water creatures called plankton. By the time the halibut are several months old, they are the size of Jessie's thumb. As they grow, workers move them into bigger tanks.

"The halibut in this tank are one year old," Grandpa says. "They've grown as big as my hand. Now they're big enough for me to buy and move out to sea cages."

"Halibut sure look weird," remarks Jessie. "Every one of them has both eyes on the same side of its head!"

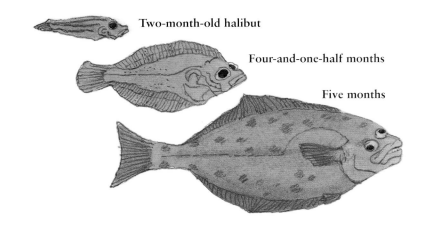

Two-month-old halibut

Four-and-one-half months

Five months

A halibut hatches with an eye on each side of its head, but by the time the fish is five months old the left eye has travelled over the top of the head and settled on the right side. Then the halibut lies hidden in the sand on the ocean bottom, waiting for smaller fish to swim by so it can eat them.

Scientists have designed a new sea cage that clamps to the ocean floor, where groundfish are most comfortable. Fish-farm workers can drop food down long tubes into the cages. On calm days, they can pull up the cages to check the groundfish and, when the fish are full grown, harvest them.

13

"Wow, the halibut in this tank are as big as you, Grandpa," Jessie says.

"Yes," agrees Grandpa. "We collect our eggs from these fish."

To make it easy for workers to collect eggs from this huge fish, scientists have invented an underwater cot. Workers herd the halibut onto the cot and raise it to the surface of the tank, where they quickly gather the eggs.

As fish farmers and scientists try raising different kinds of fish, such as halibut, rules will have to be made so that the fish farms don't pollute the sea and harm wild fish.

"Farming keeps our fishing way of life alive until there are lots of wild fish to catch again," says Grandpa.

"Let's find a farmed fish to eat," Jessie suggests.

"And make fish cakes," Grandpa says. "They're my favourite."

halibut

14

halibut cot

"Have you ever seen a halibut cot?" Jessie asks Dad when she arrives home in British Columbia.

"Never," he replies. "We do have fish hatcheries out here, but in many places there are still wild fish to catch."

"Are you sure people aren't catching too many?" asks Jessie.

"You've been talking to your grandpa," Dad says, "and it's a good point. My job is to stop overfishing of Pacific salmon and help them whenever I can."

"You have the best job," Jessie tells Dad. "Can I go to work with you?"

"OK," says Dad, "but get packing. Salmon cover a lot of territory. And fisheries officers like me have to keep track of all the different kinds. We travel hundreds of kilometres just to keep up with the salmon."

16

Pacific salmon mate and lay their eggs on the gravelly bottom of the same clear stream in which they were born. Then the adults die. After the eggs hatch, the young salmon grow in the shaded stream or a nearby lake for one or two years.

Fisheries officers keep an eye on salmon streams. Because salmon lay their eggs in loose gravel, officers make sure no one removes gravel from the stream beds or packs it down with heavy equipment. In some areas, fisheries workers even help the fish by raking away leaves and carefully adding fresh, loose gravel. Officers also check that no trees growing beside the streams are cut down. Trees shade the streams, and tree roots hold the soil so it doesn't fall in and muddy the water. Newly hatched salmon stay healthier in clear streams.

After one or two summers, the young salmon leave their birth streams and swim down rivers to the sea. They spend several years feasting on fish and shrimp in the Pacific Ocean. Then the adults swim back upriver, jumping rapids and small waterfalls. Each salmon knows exactly where it was born and returns to that spot, the females to lay their eggs, and the males to fertilize them.

"No one knows how the salmon find their way," Dad says.

Fisheries officers check salmon rivers carefully. If people dam one, a fishway is built around the dam as a detour for the fish. Sometimes fishways are built beside waterfalls to make the hard journey upriver easier. At the top of the fishways, fish counters record how many salmon travel each way.

ARCHWOOD SCHOOL
800 ARCHIBALD STREET
WINNIPEG, MANITOBA
R2J 0Y4

20

WOOD SCHOOL
ARCHIBALD STREET
WINNIPEG MANITOBA
R2J 0Y4

"One of the toughest parts of my job, Jessie, is patrolling river mouths where salmon rivers meet the ocean," Dad says. "That's where people like to build cities, pulpmills and big factories. And that could mean lots of pollution to poison the salmon. Limits are set and I check that they're obeyed."

In late summer, adult salmon return to the river mouths to start their hard trip upriver to mate. Ocean-going fishing boats move in for the catch.

The fisheries department decides how many salmon can be harvested and how many each boat is allowed to catch. Officers mark off "no fishing" areas so enough salmon get past the nets and upriver to mate. At any time, the officers can make the safe areas bigger so there will be salmon to fish in years to come.

23

"There's a big seiner fishing for salmon," says Dad.

"How did the crew know the salmon were there?" Jessie asks.

"They waited and watched for salmon jumping out of the water," answers Dad. "Then they set out a big, deep net that surrounded the fish. Now the crew is bringing in the fish and the net using the large drum on the back of the boat."

Fisheries officers in patrol boats ask the seiners to call in the number and kind of salmon they have caught that day. Everyone needs to work together to make sure the salmon aren't overfished.

seiner

seine net

25

A boat called a gillnetter is also used to catch returning salmon. The gillnetter lets down a fencelike net across the path of the fish. One end of the net is usually attached to the back of the boat and the other end to a big float called a buoy. The net drifts with the boat, and all big fish swimming into it are caught by their own gills. When the crew thinks the net is full, a motor helps them pull it in by wrapping the net around a drum.

A packer boat stands nearby, ready to take the fish to a factory. There they are killed, gutted, weighed, packaged and shipped to market. The heads and guts are chopped up and turned into fertilizer.

gillnetter

gillnet

buoy

27

On the way home, Jessie and Dad stop at a fishwheel. Here, salmon are caught partway upriver. The fish are alive in the wheel, so workers can handpick fish for processing. That way they can set free all young salmon heading out to sea or any rarer varieties on their way upriver.

"I'll choose one just right for eating," says Jessie as she nets a salmon off the fishwheel. "The kind Grandpa calls a keeper."

After supper, Jessie phones Grandpa.

"Hi there," she says. "We've got some great wild salmon out here, and we need your yummy fish cakes recipe for the leftovers."

Jessie's and Grandpa's Fish Cakes

Serves 2–3

You'll need:

250 mL (1 cup) cooked, flaked salmon,
    flounder (sole) or halibut

1 egg, beaten in a bowl

500 mL (2 cups) mashed potatoes

1 mL (¼ teaspoon) salt

30 mL (2 tablespoons) milk

15 mL (1 tablespoon) chopped parsley

30 mL (2 tablespoons) butter or
    60 mL (¼ cup) vegetable oil

250 mL (1 cup) breadcrumbs

a frying pan and flipper or spatula

an adult to help with the frying

1. Mix the fish, beaten egg, mashed potatoes, salt, milk and parsley in a bowl.

2. Shape the mixture into balls in your hand and then flatten them into patties.

3. Add the butter or oil to the frying pan and heat until it bubbles.

4. Dip each patty in the breadcrumbs and lay it in the hot frying pan.

5. Cook on each side 2 or 3 minutes or until the patty turns golden brown.

Serve hot.

Index

bait, 6
boats. *See* dories, gillnetters, longliners, packer boats, patrol boats, seiners, trawlers
British Columbia, 2, 16
buoys, 26-27

cod, 4
cots, halibut, 14-16
crews, 6, 24, 26. *See also* workers

dams, 20
dories, 4, 5, 8

eggs, fish, 10, 14, 18, 20
environmental concerns, 14, 18, 22
eyes, halibut, 12, 13

fertilizer, 26
fish. *See* cod, flounder, groundfish, halibut, salmon, wild fish
fish cakes, 30
fish counters, 20
fish farming, 2, 6-15
fish food, 10, 13, 20
fish packing, 8, 26, 28.
    See also harvesting

fisheries officers, 16-28
fishways, 20-21
fishwheels, 28
floats, 26-27
flounder, 4, 30

gillnets, 26-27
gillnetters, 26-27
gravel, 18
groundfish, 4-7, 13. *See also* cod, flounder, halibut
groundlines, 6, 7

halibut, 4, 8-16, 30
hand nets, 8, 28
harvesting, 13. *See also* fish packing
hatcheries, 8, 10-16

limits, 22. *See also* environmental concerns, rules
longliners, 6, 7

nets, fish, 4, 22, 24, 26, 28.
    See also gillnets, hand nets, seine nets, trawl nets
New Brunswick, 2

ocean, 6, 8, 13, 20, 22.
    See also sea
overfishing, 4, 6, 16, 24

Pacific Ocean, 20
packer boats, 26
patrol boats, 24
plankton, 10
pollution, 14, 22. *See also* environmental concerns

rapids, 20
river mouths, 22
rivers, 20-21, 22-23, 28
rules, 14. *See also* limits

salmon (Atlantic), 8, 30
salmon (Pacific), 16-30
sea, 4, 14, 20. *See also* ocean
sea cages, 8-9, 12-13
seine nets, 22-25
seiners, 22-25
streams, 18-20

tanks, fish, 10-15
trawl nets, 4-6
trawlers, 4, 5
trees, 18

waterfalls, 20
wild fish, 8, 14, 16, 29
workers, 8-9, 10-11, 13, 14, 28.
    See also crews

Dedicated to memories of Captain Small, Harry Yard, Willie White
and the Barnett family visits to the Maritimes

The authors gratefully acknowledge the assistance of Bob Clay,
Robert Cook, Gillian Lee, Matt Litvak, Joanne McCormick, Tom Moffatt,
Sue Leppington, Ann Prendergast and Ken Waiwood.

Thanks to Valerie Hussey, Ricky Englander and all the people at Kids Can Press.
Thanks to Pat Cupples, whose imaginative illustrations bring life to even the
most technical of details. A special thank you to Elizabeth MacLeod, Trudee Romanek and
Debbie Rogosin, whose editorial touches added warmth to chilled waters.

Text © 1997 Ann Love and Jane Drake
Illustrations © 1997 Pat Cupples

All rights reserved. No part of this publication may be reproduced,
stored in a retrieval system or transmitted, in any form or by any
means, without the prior written permission of Kids Can Press Ltd.
or, in case of photocopying or other reprographic copying, a license
from CANCOPY (Canadian Copyright Licensing Agency), 1 Yonge
Street, Suite 1900, Toronto, ON, M5E 1E5.

Many of the designations used by manufacturers and sellers to
distinguish their products are claimed as trademarks. Where those
designations appear in this book and Kids Can Press Ltd. was aware
of a trade mark claim, the designations have been printed in initial
capital letters.

Kids Can Press acknowledges the financial support of the Ontario
Arts Council, the Canada Council for the Arts and the Government
of Canada, through the BPIDP, for our publishing activity.

Published in Canada by
Kids Can Press Ltd.
29 Birch Avenue
Toronto, Ontario, Canada
M4V 1E2

The artwork in this book was rendered in watercolour, gouache,
graphite and coloured pencil on hot-press watercolour paper.

Edited by Debbie Rogosin and Trudee Romanek
Designed by Marie Bartholomew and Karen Powers
Printed in China

The hardcover edition of this book is smyth sewn casebound.
The paperback edition of this book is limp sewn with a drawn-on
cover.

CDN 97 0 9 8 7 6 5 4 3 2 1
CDN PA 01 0 9 8 7 6 5 4 3 2 1

Canadian Cataloguing in Publication Data

Love, Ann
    Fishing

(Canada at work)
Includes index.
ISBN 1-55074-339-2 (bound) ISBN 1-55074-919-6 (pbk.)

1. Fisheries — Canada — Juvenile literature. I. Drake, Jane. II.
Cupples, Patricia. III. Title. IV. Series.

SH223.L68 1997   j639.2'0971   C97-931188-8

Kids Can Press is a Nelvana company